D0385760

The Little Book of
CALM FOR CATS

BY STUART & LINDA MACFARLANE

Illustrated by Erika Oller

BANTAM BOOKS
LONDON · NEW YORK · TORONTO · SYDNEY · AUCKLAND

For Brian and Amanda – the coolest cats in town

*Special thanks to Macavity, Midnight, Mistoffelees
and Mungojerrie for their dedicated research* – S. & L.M.

For my beautiful boy, Romeo – E.O.

THE LITTLE BOOK OF CALM FOR CATS
A BANTAM BOOK: 0553 81339 0

First publication in Great Britain

PRINTING HISTORY
Bantam Books edition published 2000

1 3 5 7 9 10 8 6 4 2

Bantam Books are published by Transworld Publishers,
61-63 Uxbridge Road, London W5 5SA,
a division of The Random House Group Ltd,
in Australia by Random House Australia (Pty) Ltd,
20 Alfred Street, Milsons Point, Sydney, NSW 2061, Australia,
in New Zealand by Random House New Zealand Ltd,
18 Poland Road, Glenfield, Auckland 10, New Zealand
and in South Africa by Random House (Pty) Ltd,
Endulini, 5a Jubilee Road, Parktown 2193, South Africa.

Printed in Singapore

At the start of each and every day look in the mirror,
hold your tail high, and recite the following mantra:

> *I'm a dynamic superhero,*
> *I shall rid the world of mice,*
> *I shall learn to fly like a bird,*
> *I shall teach my human tricks,*
> *I shall conquer vicious dogs.*
> *But first I'll take my nap.*

Don't do anything today

that can be put off until another life.

From time to time engage in the seemingly trivial pursuit of frantically chasing a ball of wool.

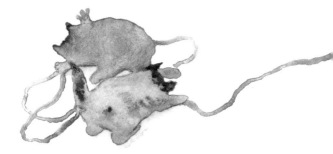

This frivolous activity will absorb all
your negative energy and fill you with a
wonderful sense of inner peace.

Scratching is a powerful stress-relieving technique. For maximum benefit practise on the most expensive wallpaper, curtains and carpets. At all costs avoid scratch pads provided by humans as these will send your stress levels soaring.

Cool Cats Rule:

Cat Maxim on Existence: *I sleep therefore I am.*

Cat Maxim on Sleeping: *Sometimes twenty-four hours a day is just too little.*

Cat Maxim on Adversity: *When in trouble purr and look cute. When in serious trouble blame the dog.*

Cat Maxim on Curiosity: *Curiosity never killed anything except a few hours of time.*

Cat Maxim on Exercise: *No strain – no pain.*

Cat Maxim on Worry: *Do it in your next life.*

Cat Maxim on Relaxation: *A good rest must never be hurried.*

Cat Maxim on Life: *Life is easy, and then you nap.*

Daily Agenda for an ultra-calm life:

00:00-05:27 *Sleep on bed*
05:27-05:30 *Wake your human*
05:30-05:40 *Breakfast*
05:40-11:00 *Sleep in favourite box*
11:00-11:01 *Exercise (optional)*
11:01-13:00 *Sleep in underwear drawer*
13:00-13:10 *Lunch*
13.10-18.00 *Sleep under television*
18:00-18:15 *Dinner*
18:15-00:00 *Sleep on chair*

Climb into a box – any box.

Inside you will discover a mystical place
where you can escape from all the stresses
and strains of the world.

Avoid the company of dogs –
they are vexatious to the spirit.

How to enjoy nine stress-free lives.

Life 1 – Sleep

Life 2 – Sleep

Life 3 – Sleep

Life 4 – Sleep

Life 5 – Sleep

Life 6 – Sleep

Life 7 – Sleep

Life 8 – Sleep

Life 9 – Catch up on everything
you should have done.

Anxiety Warning: Those delicious-looking fish swishing about in the big glass bowl are impossible to catch – don't frustrate yourself by even trying.

Who am I?
What is the meaning of life?
Do cats exist on other planets?
Don't worry over such trivial questions, instead focus
on the truly important.
In a drawer?
On top of the fridge?
Under the TV?

Where *should* you sleep next?

Never attack a hedgehog.

Find the most comfortable chair in the house
and make it your own.

Go there regularly to relax and vanquish
the stresses of life.

Viciously lash out at any human who dares
to disturb your peaceful meditation.

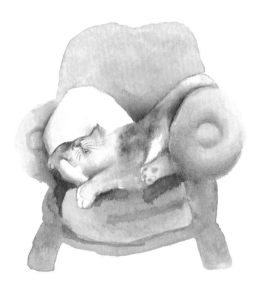

Lie in a warm, comfortable position and listen to the soft soothing sound of your own purring.

Meditate on its calming rhythm and allow yourself to drift gently into a deep sleep.

Conserve your energy. When you crave attention one doleful look into your human's eyes will have greater effect than many minutes of stressful meowing.

Nurture the ability to look pathetic and your human will forever be your slave.

Avoid vets!

Take regular breaks from your rigorous sleeping
duties to sit quietly in a warm, sunny spot
and simply enjoy the peace.

Practise the art of feng shui – rearrange your human's possessions to enhance your mood. Knock car keys and jewellery onto the floor, preferably into a dark corner out of sight, then stretch out and let your mind relax in a clutter-free environment.

At the end of a long nerve-racking day relax and reflect on all your achievements – wallpaper scratched, curtains scaled and one piece of string thoroughly chased. Celebrate these small successes. They make life worthwhile.

Don't worry about your next life.
Relax in the present
and the future will be *purrfect*.